Pictures of the Civil War

★

FIVE UNION SOLDIERS' SKETCHBOOKS

BY

Caroline Luther and Susan F. Saidenberg

THE GILDER LEHRMAN
INSTITUTE *of* AMERICAN HISTORY

NEW YORK 2010

Soldier Sketchbooks from the Gilder Lehrman Collection

Berckhoff, Henry, Sketchbook of 19 watercolors, c. 1861-1863.
(The Gilder Lehrman Institute of American History, GLC06106)

Anonymous, "A FEW SCENES In the life of a 'Sojer' in the Mass 44th 1863," c. 1862-1863.
(The Gilder Lehrman Institute of American History, GLC08200)

Park, Frank E., Sketchbook of 34 watercolors and 8 charcoal images, c. 1864.
(The Gilder Lehrman Institute of American History, GLC03537)

Stauffer, David McNeely, 66-page sketchbook, c. 1864.
(The Gilder Lehrman Collection, GLC07713.01)

Mansfield, John W., Book of Military Scraps, 1865.
(The Gilder Lehrman Collection, GLC09041)

Cover illustration: Soldiers on picket duty, illustration from the sketchbook of Frank E. Park, c. 1864.
(The Gilder Lehrman Institute of American History, GLC03537p20)

All images are from the Gilder Lehrman Collection of the Gilder Lehrman Institute of American History.

Copyright 2010
The Gilder Lehrman Institute of American History
19 W. 44th St., Ste. 500, New York, NY 10036

ISBN: 978-1-932821-82-6

Contents

2   Introduction

5   Henry Berckhoff

16   Anonymous Creator of "George"

27   Frank E. Park

34   David McNeely Stauffer

41   John W. Mansfield

48   Influences on the Artists

52   To Learn More

53   Acknowledgements

Introduction

How did the Civil War look to those who fought in it? The pictures in this book, drawn from the Gilder Lehrman Collection, were created by five Union soldiers during the war, all of them amateur artists at the time. They privately recorded their experiences in scrapbooks carried through battle and shared, perhaps, with only their closest comrades and select loved ones. They sketched heroic scenes of soldiers fighting and humorous pictures highlighting the absurdities of war. They tried to make sense of some of the war's most horrific battles by reimagining famous images created by professional artists and photographers, borrowing from them various themes and forms of composition. These unique visual representations of the Civil War experience include watercolor scenes of battles, pencil sketches of camp life, cartoons with sight gags, and images of African Americans that are remarkably free of the stereotyping common at the time.

Henry Berckhoff, the unknown artist behind the "George" comic, Frank E. Park, David McNeely Stauffer, and John W. Mansfield came from diverse backgrounds. They served in different units, and they followed even more divergent paths after the war. Berckhoff, a German immigrant from New York, stayed in the military until 1894. The mystery comic-strip artist from the 44th (or 45th) Massachusetts Infantry most likely returned home to Boston after his regiment disbanded in mid-1863, not realizing that his artistic creations were decades ahead of their time. Park took over his family's thriving South Boston masonry and construction business. Stauffer, who dropped out of Franklin and Marshall College to become Admiral David Porter's assistant, later traveled the world as an engineer. Mansfield, who was fifteen when he enlisted, went to Paris to study art.

The work of these five artists provides a powerful counterpoint to the illustrations made by the dozens of wartime professionals, whose images have long formed the basis of the war's visual legacy. As soon as the war broke out, lithographers and printers rushed to produce images of battles and portraits of great military leaders that helped reinforce pride in the Union cause. These prints were reproduced in newspapers and sold as single images on the streets for a penny to an American public hungry for news of the progress of the war and the fate of their loved ones.

Our five soldiers did not create their images for commercial publication. Rather, their work was a private response to the war. As such, their images have an immediacy undiluted by the desire to convince or reassure, unlike the letters hundreds of thousands of soldiers sent home. So few soldiers had the desire or skill to convey their reactions in images; our soldiers created pictures to help them remember and make sense of what they had seen. What makes their work so fascinating for students and teachers is that it offers glimpses into very personal spaces. Presumably, very few people saw any drawings by Berckhoff, Park, and the artist behind the George comic. Mansfield worked as an artist after the war, and Stauffer, an engineer, kept personal sketchbooks similar to his wartime creations for the rest of his life. The two honed their already evident skills as the war went on.

The five soldiers shared an interest in battles and daily life in camp. Yet the drawings they created differed in style and exaction. Berckhoff drew only battles and landscapes he had seen, and his drawings serve as a unique visual history of his regiment. Park focused mainly on what he had seen in serene watercolors and charcoal sketches, breaking form to create a symbolic homage to the fallen at Antietam and a personal version of the popular Currier & Ives "The Soldier's Grave." Stauffer was fascinated by the people and military technology he saw, and his sketchbooks contain page after page of the ships, cannons, knots, insignia, and people, including nuns, and free African Americans he encountered in his travels up and down the Mississippi. Mansfield seemed to be practicing his skills as a draftsman in preparation for his career as an artist. The anonymous creator of the "George" sketches produced the most inventive and groundbreaking visual representation of the war. Drawing upon his biting sense of humor, he created a series of linked cartoons to tell a story that lampooned the seriousness of war and the drudgery of camp life.

Selections from each of the five soldiers' sketchbooks are reproduced in the following chapters, along with brief biographies chronicling their war service and later lives. How do we know about the soldiers? During the war, their military service records were kept on muster cards, and these cards were later collected and filed by the Pension Office, a federal agency within the Department of the Interior. These records provide intimate details of soldiers' lives, including their medical records and paperwork associated with leaves of absence. From Berckhoff's pension file, for example, we learn that he was wounded in 1864 and then requested a furlough in New York to be closer to his family. His leave denied, Berckhoff wrote a poignant letter to the surgeon general stating, "I have served two years & have never been home. I am informed by my sister that my mother is seriously ill & that if I wish to see her alive I must come home this fall." A September 27, 1864, order by the Secretary of War granting his transfer can be found two pages later in his file; by March 1865, Berckhoff was summoned to Washington, D.C., to stand trial for desertion. Mansfield's, Park's, and Stauffer's lives were partially reconstructed through a National Park Service database, which provides some information on the movements of their regiments; a variety of turn-of-the-century *Who's Who*–type publications and regimental histories that have recently been digitized by Google; obituaries available through Google News and the National Endowment for the Humanities' Chronicling America project; and the David McNeely Stauffer papers at the New York Public Library. Possible identities of George's creator have been reconstructed using similar sources; in particular, an exceptionally good regimental history of the 44th Massachusetts published in the late 1880s, and the wartime letters of Zenas T. Haines, a *Boston Herald* reporter who was stationed with the 44th, that have been reprinted and annotated in William C. Harris's *In the Country of the Enemy*.

In addition to the many diaries and letters by Civil War soldiers, which have been mined by many researchers, and photographs, which were often staged by professionals, the personal and previously unpublished images in this book will lead to new understandings of soldiers' experiences—150 years after the war began.

Henry Berckhoff
1840–1905

Born in Leidingen, Germany; moved to New York

Eighth New York Volunteer Regiment (First German Rifles), April 1861–April 1863

Fifth Regiment, New York Veteran Infantry, October 1863–August 1865

Various units, U.S. Regular Army, 1868–1894

Born in Leidingen, Brunswick, Germany, Henry Berckhoff was twenty years old on April 23, 1861, when he left his job as a clerk and his home with his mother in New York City to enlist as a private in the Eighth New York Volunteer Infantry, a regiment made up mostly of German immigrants. When the Eighth New York, also known as the First German Rifles, marched off to Washington, D.C., on May 27, New Yorkers lined the streets to wish them luck. Berckhoff recorded this event in the first of nineteen pencil and watercolor images documenting more than two years of battles, marches, and quiet moments in camp.

The Eighth New York was commanded by Louis Blenker, a German exile who had participated in the 1848 revolution. Blenker's taste for the finer things and love of military pageantry attracted attention from the press and generals alike, including Gen. George B. McClellan, who was a frequent visitor to the Eighth New York's camp outside Washington, D.C. Berckhoff must have been aware of the widespread attention to his regiment, including that of Alfred Waud, who sketched the war for the *New York Illustrated News* and *Harper's Weekly*, and drew a scene identified as Blenker's camp on Thanksgiving in 1861.

Unlike two of the other soldier artists whose work appears in this book, Berckhoff drew only what he saw. The Eighth New York was held in reserve at the First Battle of Bull Run but covered the retreat of Union forces on July 21, 1861, in a manner that earned them praise. Berckhoff's sketch of the retreat shows Union scouts and sharpshooters standing in front of orderly lines of infantrymen whom Confederate soldiers seemingly fail to notice. Berckhoff's other battle scenes include the June 1862 Battle of Cross Keys, which features bloodied Union soldiers in the foreground being attended to by their comrades; Second Bull Run, a smoke-filled affair; a cavalry skirmish near Alden, a confusing scrum of men and horses; and another skirmish near Haymarket, with Union forces on a gallant charge amidst burning buildings. Most of Berckhoff's sketches are devoted to peaceful scenes: building Camp Blenker, an almost idyllic morning at Camp Hunter's Chappel, soldiers huddling around a campfire while a nighttime thunderstorm rages, various marches, and a depiction of soldiers heading home.

After ending his two-year commitment in April 1863, Berckhoff returned to New York City to reenlist almost immediately in the Fifth Regiment, New York Veterans Infantry. He was sent to Virginia to serve in the Overland Campaign and was wounded in action by a rifle ball in August 1864. While recuperating in a hospital in Washington, D.C., he requested a transfer to New York City to see his dying mother. This somehow sparked a desertion case, but was cleared up by August 1865, when Berckhoff was dishonorably discharged.

Whatever his ambitions before 1861, Berckhoff was in and out of the army from 1868 until 1894, most likely serving in the Indian Wars. His service record is confusing, but it appears he served in the First Regiment U.S. Regular Army until 1876, then served another stint from 1878 until his retirement in 1894 in the

21st Regiment Infantry, U.S. Regular Army. He served again in the Eighth Regiment Infantry, U.S. Regular Army, and never rose very far through the ranks. In his 1905 request for a disability pension, the sixty-four-year-old Berckhoff reported rheumatism, failing eyesight, weak lungs, and "general disability due to old age." Though the government doctor who examined him recommended that he receive a pension of $8 a month, his request was denied. He lived his last years at various addresses on the Upper West Side of Manhattan, presumably unmarried and childless, dying on an unknown date, never having received the pension he most likely deserved. If he kept any other sketchbooks, they have never made their way to the archives.

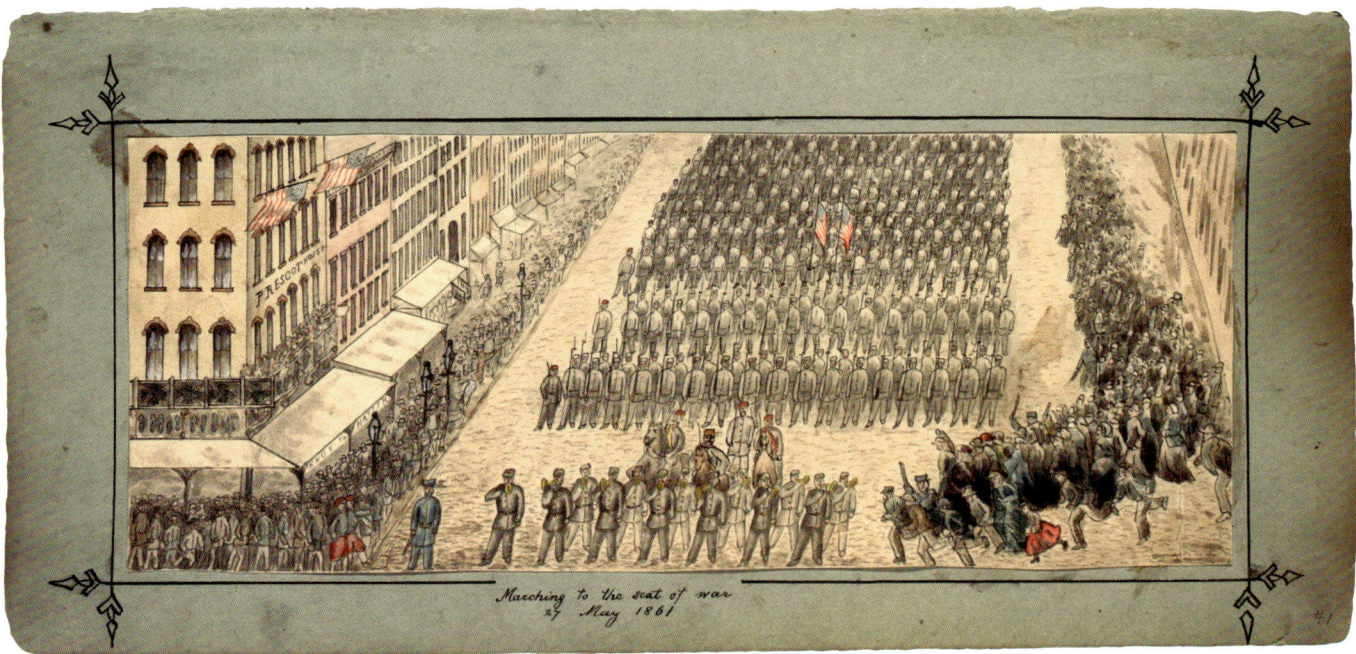

The Eighth New York Volunteer Infantry, also known as the First German Rifles, was commanded by Col. Louis Blenker. When they "marched to the seat of war" (Washington, D.C.) on May 27, 1861, German Americans and other New Yorkers lined Broadway to cheer on the soldiers. Once in Washington, the Eighth New York made a strong impression. Unlike many volunteer regiments, it had an artillery unit and medical detachment with ambulances. The soldiers also had two different uniforms: the regular blue as well as a distinctive gray for parades and other ceremonial occasions. This image and the ones that follow in this section are from the Gilder Lehrman Collection, GLC06106.

Berckhoff captured both quiet and grand moments in his sketches. A lone soldier patrols the banks of the Potomac in the top image on this page, while the First Battle of Bull Run appears on the bottom. The Eighth New York was held in reserve at the First Battle of Bull Run, but assisted in covering the chaotic retreat of the Union forces on July 21, 1861. A pointing man, most likely Blenker, commands orderly lines of soldiers from the Eighth New York while sharpshooters hold their posts.

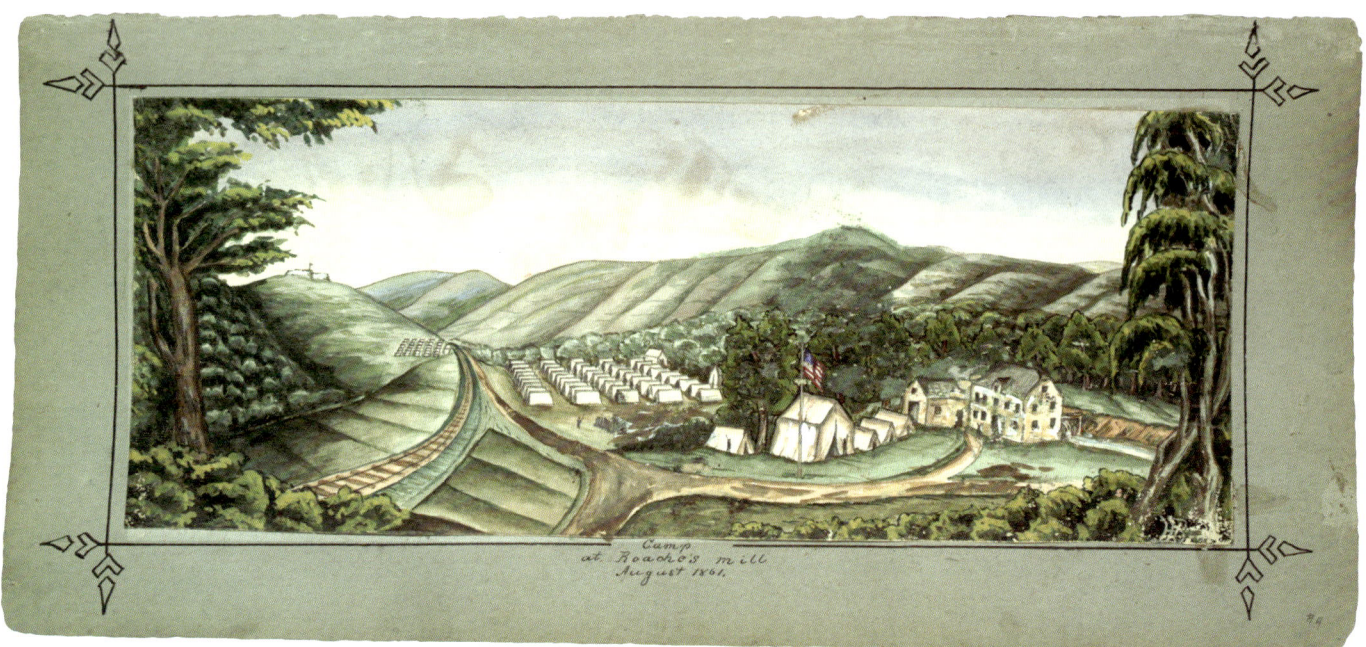

The Eighth New York set up camp in a distinctive fashion. The soldiers' tents were arranged in orderly rows with lanes of fir and cedar trees separating each regiment in the division. The Eighth New York's Washington, D.C. camp was a tourist attraction, with McClellan a regular visitor.

There is a poignancy in the ordinary details of Berckhoff's camp scenes. In "Morning Scene at Camp Hunter's Chappel," soldiers wash their clothes and themselves, cook food, and build a fire. A mirror is hung from a tree so a soldier can carefully comb his hair; pots and pans are arranged for cooking; and a tree stump is used as a chair. Camp life was punctuated with military duties such as patrolling, seen in "Attack on the Outposts near Annondale, Va."

PICTURES OF THE CIVIL WAR | 9

Gen. Blenker's fatal fall
at Salem
7 April 1862.

Crossing the Shenandoah river
on pontoons at Berryville
17 April 1862

Blenker's troops got caught in an unusual spring snowstorm in Virginia in April 1862 and wandered for ten days without tents or adequate supplies. Brigadier General William Rosecrans was sent to find them and help them cross the Shenandoah. By the time the Eighth New York was found, Blenker had fallen and sustained injuries that would eventually kill him in late 1863, and his men were so weak that they performed poorly in their next campaign.

Weakened from their wanderings through the snow, the Eighth New York marched to the site of their next battle. Berckhoff captured their weariness in the above images, which make the march appear endless.

In order to reach the battlefield and set up camp, Civil War soldiers often took on the tasks of construction workers, as Berckhoff's regiment did on the way to Cross Keys. By many accounts, the Eighth New York fought terribly at Cross Keys on June 8, 1862. The Confederate victory there and at Port Republic forced a Union retreat. Soon after, General Franz Sigel arrived in the Shenandoah and Blenker was ordered to return to Washington.

The Second Battle of Bull Run, fought on the same ground as First Bull Run, was a much larger battle. Berckhoff captured this in "Battle on Manassas Plains," a smoke-filled scene of line after line of soldiers—a perspective that minimizes the day's death and destruction. "Cavalry skirmish near Alden" stands in contrast, appearing more like a fistfight than a meeting of two armies.

In November 1862, almost all of the town of Haymarket, Virginia, was consumed by fires set by Union troops in an attempt to root out a Confederate sniper. Berckhoff documented the destruction in one of his most dramatic and violent sketches. "Rail road guard near Brooks Station" stands in stark contrast, with a single soldier patrolling a pristine, snowy landscape.

Berckhoff created another scene of quiet misery in "Bivouac at Dumfries," with soldiers huddled around a fire as a thunderstorm rages while others sleep unprotected in the rain. "Homeward bound," which shows soldiers leaving Virginia by all available forms of transportation after the Eighth New York's service was up, juxtaposes the nation's past, represented by horses, wagons, and sailing ships with new technologies such as steamships and railroads, which evoke a vision of the future and westward expansion.

Anonymous Creator of "George"

From the Boston area

44th Massachusetts Volunteer Militia, August 1862–May 1863

The anonymously authored "A FEW SCENES in the life of a 'sojer' in the Mass 44th 1863" chronicles the exploits of a character called George, or sometimes Gorge. George and his friends—who include two band members from the 45th Massachusetts named Whit and Collyer—steal General Beauregard's horse, encounter freed slaves, and serve on picket duty. George comes close to being eaten by an alligator, is saved by Whit or Collyer while on picket duty, and gets treated with the water cure after sustaining a foot injury. According to "A FEW SCENES," it was an exciting nine-month tour for this group from Boston who saw action in New Bern, North Carolina, between October 1862 and June 1863.

None of the most outrageous stories depicted in this comic are confirmed in any of regimental histories and diaries written by members of the 44th, an unusually cohesive and educated group who left behind a wealth of published material about their service. Several incidents that appeared in print, however, could have provided inspiration for George's adventures. The men of Company D, a mischievous group, woke up one night to an exploding stove in their barracks, the result of a prank involving gunpowder. Soldiers from Company I, meanwhile, perfected the art of throwing hardtack at each other. Bored members of the invalid guard piled into a boat, stranded one of their comrades who couldn't swim on shore, and convinced him that the Confederates were coming.

No names are attached to these incidents, and we're left to speculate about George's identity. Clearly, the creator of "A FEW SCENES" was clever. He had a dark sense of humor and love of sight gags. He was well-versed in popular culture, reimagining *Harper's Weekly* sketches and using slang. And he loved cartoons, then a new art form. The first comic book was published in the United States in 1842, a translation of Rudolphe Töpffer's *The Adventures of Mr. Obadiah Oldbuck. Journey to the Gold Diggins by Jeremiah Saddlebags*, written by Americans James and Donald Read, followed in 1849. The unknown artist may have been trying to recreate these comic books, but his limited drawing skills prevented him from doing so. These same limited drawing skills may have led him to experiment with close-up reaction scenes, something not seen in published cartoons of the day, producing a finished product that feels contemporary.

Officers from the 44th Massachusetts Volunteer Militia, photograph, c. 1862-1863. (The Gilder Lehrman Institute of American History, GLC003395.02)

Ninety-eight men named George served in the 44th Massachusetts Regiment, ninety-eight possible suspects. Did someone named George even draw these cartoons? Who was the audience for these cartoons? Did the artist even show them to anyone?

Could our mystery artist be twenty-year-old George W. Hight, who drew "an excellent sketch of our situation and defences at Washington" according to Zenas T. Haines, a *Boston Herald* reporter serving with Hight in Company D? Haines sent a sketch in one of his many dispatches to his editor, noting that one could "take pleasure in showing to any friend of the 44th regiment" the sketch—making it sound like something out of the ordinary and possibly funny. Adding more evidence to this theory is Hight's March 27, 1914 *Boston Globe* obituary mentioning that he was a native of Nantucket who split his time between Boston and New York as a lumber merchant. "A FEW SCENES" turned up in the late 1990s near Cape Cod, casting even more suspicion on Hight.

Or is George Henry Hobart our man? In a sketch showing "Gorge and his friends" from the 44th "returning to Newbern after the Battle of Goldsboro," reprinted on p. 24, the initials "G.H.H." are visible on a bedraggled soldier's backpack. Hobart, who enlisted as a private with the 44th at age twenty and hailed from Newton, Massachusetts, re-enlisted in the 42nd Massachusetts on the Fourth of July 1864 for a 100-day tour that took him near Washington, D.C. We know that the creator of "A FEW SCENES" enjoyed an extensive military life allowing him to find the dark humor in it, and took the time to create an unusual record of his service. It also seems that Hobart spent some time in North Carolina while ill—his pension is listed in a chapter about sick reports—and the character George turns up in the infirmary for a while after cutting his foot.

Perhaps George's creator wasn't named George at all. Perhaps he didn't even serve in the 44th. The 45th Massachusetts had a similar service record to the 44th, with recruits from the Boston area arriving in New Bern less than a month after the 44th. On several occasions, two characters named Whit and Collyer, both identified as members of the 45th Massachusetts and as members of the regimental band, appear in sketches. Collyer is John L. Collyer, a twenty-four-year-old clerk from Gloucester. Whit could be either John D. or Henry C. Whitcomb, twenty-eight and thirty-one-year-old brothers from Boston who worked in the printing business and were detailed to the regimental band. Both were abolitionists and important figures in publishing: John, a longtime employee of the influential *Boston Evening Transcript* who corresponded with William Lloyd Garrison, and Henry, an electrotyper and engraver who worked on bookplates for *Uncle Tom's Cabin*. "A FEW SCENES" was drawn inside an 1840s printer's catalog. Could Henry or John be our mystery artist?

For now, the question of George's—and our artist's—identity remains unanswered. The continuing digitization of Civil War records could make a future identification possible. In the meantime, we can marvel at our unknown artist's wit, laugh at his jokes, and wonder who he was.

Picket duty was at once hazardous and monotonous. Here, the creator of "A FEW SCENES" employs the first of many sight gags in an attempt to illustrate what the job entailed before pointing out one of its hardships: long stretches of hunger. This image and the ones that follow in this section are from the Gilder Lehrman Collection, GLC08200.

General Beauregard was nowhere near New Bern when the 44th served there, and if any of the 1,000-plus soldiers in the 44th attempted to steal a Confederate officer's horse, the numerous regimental histories are silent on the subject.

Rudolphe Töpffer, a Swiss graphic artist, invented the comic strip in 1827, and his most famous comic book, *The Adventures of Obadiah Oldbuck*, was reprinted in an obscure New York newspaper in 1842. It's impossible to know whether the creator of George ever read it, but his multi-panel sequences, shifting perspectives, and action-packed scenes far surpass comics then in print and anticipate the modern comic book form by decades, as this sequence with an alligator demonstrates.

This is the second time George's comrades come to his rescue in "A FEW SCENES." The first, reprinted on page 26, occurs after George is captured by rebels while on picket duty.

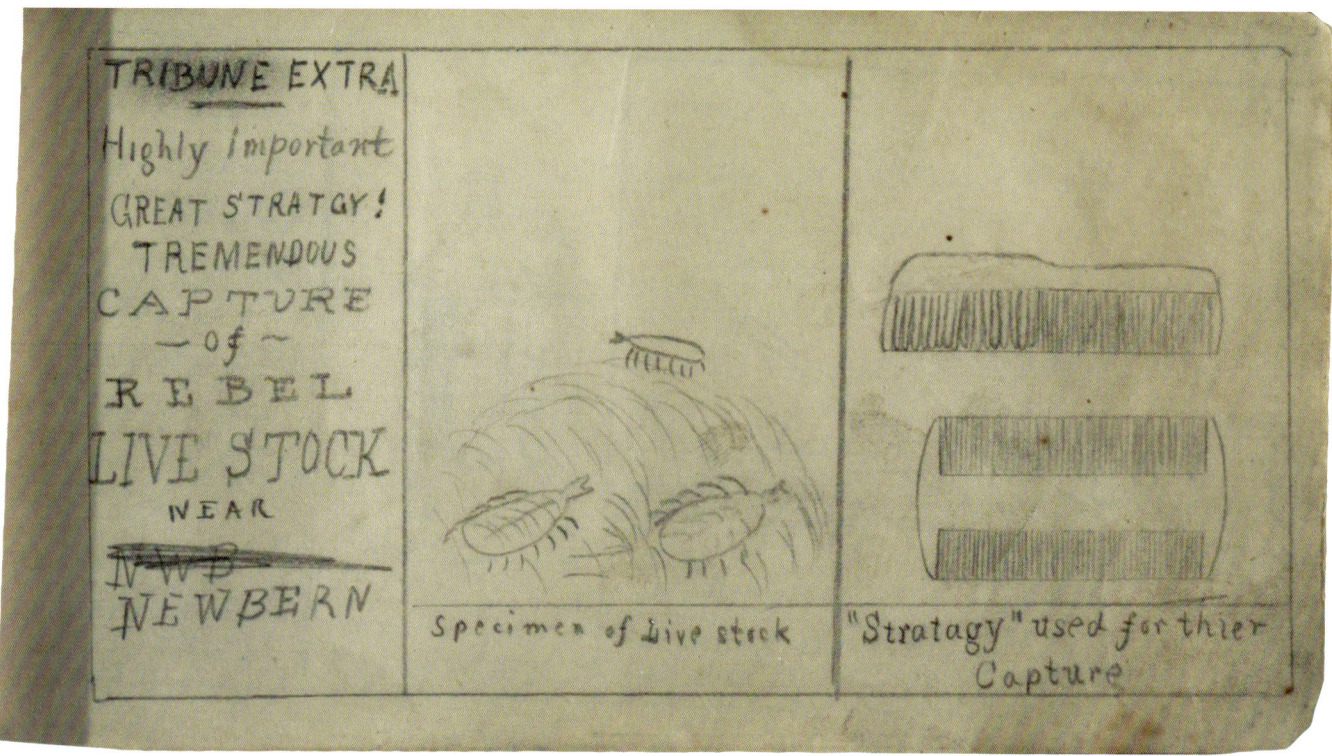

The artist of "A FEW SCENES" devoted a fair amount of attention to creating humorous illustrations of newspaper headlines and reimagining battle scenes by professionals such as Currier & Ives and published in *Harper's Weekly* and *Frank Leslie's Illustrated Newspaper*. Here, misspelled headlines announce the destruction of an important bridge and the capture of rebel livestock: lice, a scourge of Union and Confederate troops.

A *Boston Herald* reporter served with the 44th and sent regular dispatches to his editor. The exaggerated reports lampooned in these sketches are credited to the *Boston Journal*, a rival paper whose wartime correspondent, Charles Carleton Coffin, was one of the most famous Civil War reporters.

The battle of Goldsboro was the 44th's largest campaign, involving a fifteen-mile forced march over sandy roads. Here, the artist reimagined a *Harper's* engraving of the battle in a more cartoonish—and likely more realistic—depiction, and illustrated the fatigue George and his comrades felt on the long march back from the ultimately unsuccessful campaign.

Bull Run and Fredericksburg were fought before the 44th was assembled, but the artist of "A FEW SCENES," like Frank Park and John Mansfield, sketched battles he hadn't seen. It's possible that he was injured soon after the battle of Goldsboro, as six pages are devoted to scenes where George endures a painful cut and even more painful treatment in the infirmary. No new scenes from New Bern appear after the injury, as the artist turned his attention to pun-filled recreations of famous battles.

Who was the creator of "A FEW SCENES"? He provides clues to his friends' identities—Collyer is John L. Collyer, and Whit is either John D. or Henry C. Whitcomb, all from the Massachusetts 45th, also stationed in New Bern—and possibly his own, with a bedraggled figure on p. 24 bearing the initials "G.H.H." on his backpack.

Frank E. Park
1835–1904

South Boston, Massachusetts

Sixth Massachusetts Volunteer Militia, 1864

View of the White House with soldiers on patrol, photograph by Mathew Brady, c. 1861-1865. (The Gilder Lehrman Institute of American History, 05111.02.0039)

At age twenty-nine, Frank E. Park enlisted in the Andrew Light Infantry, a 100-day volunteer militia from Massachusetts, in early July 1864. The Andrew Light Infantry, or Sixth Massachusetts Volunteer Militia, was first sent to Arlington Heights, Virginia, to guard Fort C.F. Smith, then transferred to Fort Delaware to guard a camp of 7,000 Confederate prisoners. Park mustered out with his comrades on October 27 in Readville, Massachusetts, having seen no action in a campaign that even the Sixth's regimental historian called "not eventful." Yet the Sixth's service was important, the regimental historian argued, because 100-day militias "held important positions until new men came in, to take the places of those whose term had expired. . . . Besides, many of them could leave important positions at home for so brief a period, who could not have been obtained for a longer time."[1]

This could have been the case with Park, a mason and contractor from South Boston. A profile in a 1900 book about South Boston and its leading residents portrays Park as a well-to-do businessman heavily involved in civic organizations and Republican politics. Park also served as commander of his local Grand Army of the Republic post, seemingly having enjoyed his time in the military, despite what one longtime Union soldier, writing to his sister in 1864, said about 100-day militias: "I am glad they are raising so many 100 day men. I think now is the time they need if ever, but they will find there is no fun in soldiering that length of time. . . . The first few months of a soldiers life is the hardest there is, the time he thinks of home."[2]

Park's sketches—thirty-four watercolors and eight in pencil—chronicle the Andrew Light Infantry's movements from Readville, Mass., to northern Virginia and back, supporting the regimental historian's claim that Park and his comrades saw little action. In beautifully composed scenes, Park depicts his regiment's departure, camp life, and guard duty, and various landscapes around him, including scenes from the mid-Atlantic coastline looking out to sea. If he was homesick, Park's sketches betray nothing of it.

---

1 John Wesley Hanson, *Historical Sketch of the Old Sixth Regiment of Massachusetts Volunteers* (Boston: Lee and Shepard, 1866), 305.
2 Dolphus Damuth to Ida, June 2, 1864. The Gilder Lehrman Institute of American History, GLC03523.14.58.

The Andrews Light Infantry (ALI), like most Massachusetts regiments, trained at Camp Meigs in Readville. Here, Park depicts the ALI's June 1864 departure and sketches characters who appear in later images. This image and the ones that follow in this section are from the Gilder Lehrman Collection, GLC03537.

The Andrews Light Infantry traveled by boat to Arlington Heights, Virginia, to guard Fort C.F. Smith. Park sketched several images of his regiment's sea voyage and the Upper Potomac.

Seemingly influenced by photographic technique—he posed his subjects to face him, as they would have done for a camera—Park created several scenes of everyday life. Here, a supply team rests, and soldiers relax in camp, facing forward.

A far cry from the version of picket duty depicted in "A FEW SCENES," (see p. 18), Park's sketches again employ photographic technique, with subjects facing the viewer.

PICTURES OF THE CIVIL WAR | 31

Park captured some of the grandeur of his surroundings in these scenes of Washington, D.C., and Fort C.F. Smith.

In two grim sketches, Park illustrated the war's costs. His view of the Antietam battlefield is much darker than that of Currier & Ives and John Mansfield (p. 51). The sketch of a soldier standing in front of two of his fallen comrades' tombstones is reminiscent of "The Soldier's Memorial," one in a series of customizable Currier & Ives prints that included blank spaces for families to write in their dead soldiers' names.

PICTURES OF THE CIVIL WAR | 33

David McNeely Knox Stauffer 1845–1913

Lancaster, Pennsylvania

Second Pennsylvania Emergency Regiment, 1862

Independent Battery of Pennsylvania, 1863-1864

First District, Mississippi Squadron, 1864-1865

Seventeen-year-old Franklin and Marshall College student David McNeely Knox Stauffer left school in September 1862 to volunteer with the Second Pennsylvania Emergency Regiment, a short-lived militia raised to resist General Robert E. Lee's invasion of Maryland, and returned to school in the winter having seen action at Antietam. In June 1863, he joined Nevin's Independent Battery of the Pennsylvania Light Artillery, serving in Philadelphia and Harpers Ferry before mustering out in January 1864 to work with the Engineering Corps of the Pennsylvania and Port DuPont Railroad.

In February, Stauffer continued his service by joining the navy as Admiral David Porter's master's mate in the Mississippi Squadron. The Squadron patrolled the Mississippi and its tributaries and helped supply Union troops in the west. His ship, USS *Alexandria*, carried messages between Porter, Admiral David Farragut on the Mississippi River, and General Edward Canby, who was in charge of land forces. Approaching his new job like a college course, Stauffer filled his 1864 sketchbook with meticulous notes on everything from schedules to the various flags used to signal boat maneuvers to uniform insignias. Stauffer, who studied engineering at Franklin and Marshall, seemed fascinated by all aspects of military technology, and carefully sketched cross-sections and schematic drawings of large guns, as well as ammunition. His sketchbook also reflects an interest in the other vessels of the Mississippi Squadron, and in the people he encountered in Louisiana, including free blacks.

Stauffer didn't go back to college after the war, choosing instead to begin a career as a civil engineer. He pioneered several construction techniques on railroad bridges throughout Pennsylvania and New Jersey, and worked on a tunnel in Boston, grain elevators near Philadelphia, and the Wichita, Kansas, water supply system before becoming editor and part owner of *Engineering News*. He developed an interest in copper and steel engraving, designing book plates for several libraries and publishing a four-volume history of American engraving in 1907. A member of numerous prestigious clubs and societies, including the Grolier Club, the Union League Club, the Century Club, and the Sons of the American Revolution, Stauffer was heavily involved in civic life in Philadelphia and New York. He never lost interest in his own drawing, keeping sketchbooks into the 1880s and possibly until his death in 1913 in Yonkers, New York.

Naval officers, photograph, c. 1861-1865. (The Gilder Lehrman Institute of American History, GLC05111.02.1418)

Stauffer, an engineering student, devoted a great deal of attention to military technology in his sketches. This scale sketch of an Armstrong gun—shown being operated by Zouaves, soldiers who adopted the name and the North African–inspired uniforms of the French army in Algeria—provides a sense of its size. This image and the ones that follow in this section are from the Gilder Lehrman Collection, GLC07713.01.

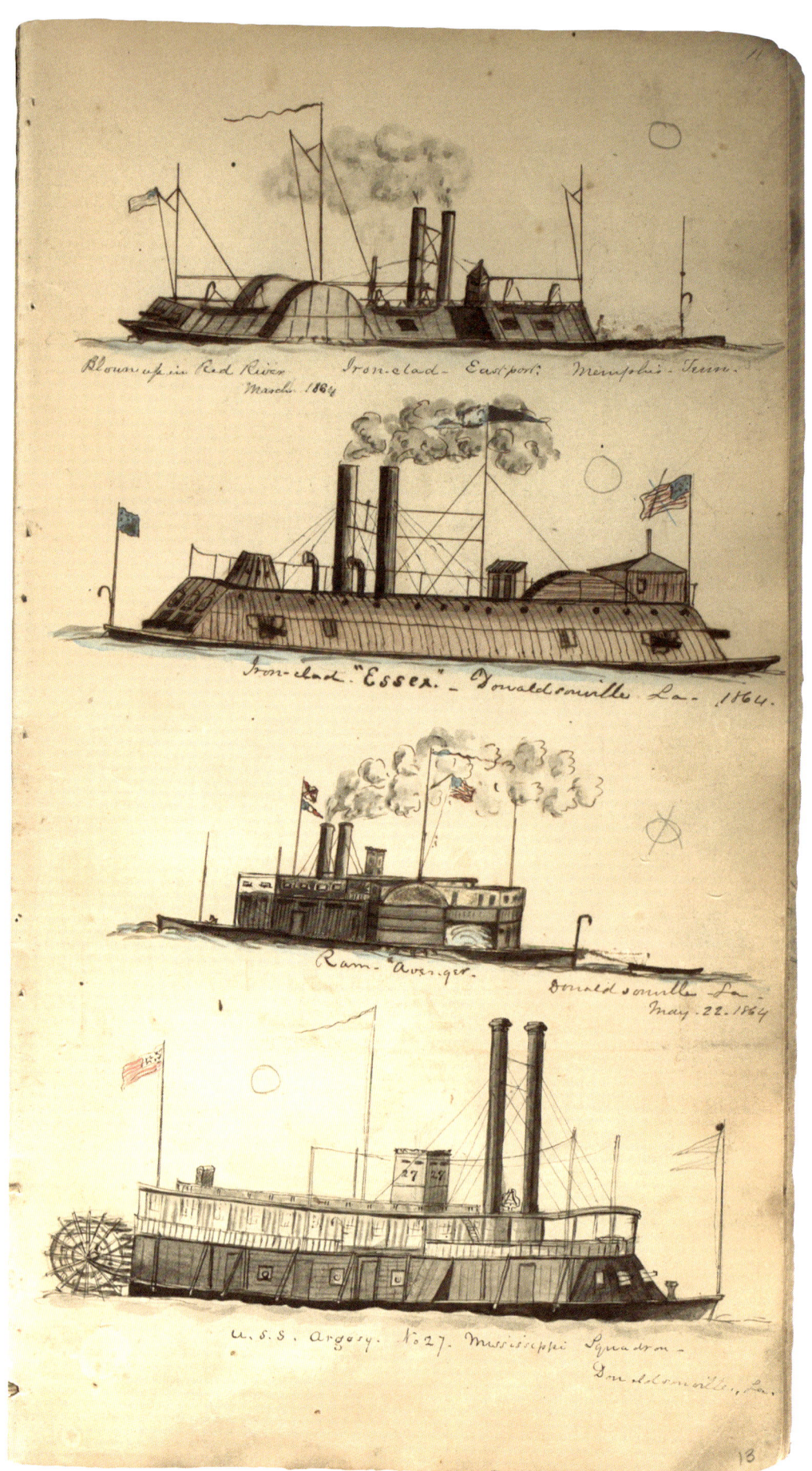

Stauffer sketched page after page of ships in the Mississippi Squadron, the ragtag Union navy fleet that patrolled the nation's western rivers. An anomaly from its creation—it was originally part of the Union army—the Mississippi Squadron was made up of ships customized to "brown water" (as opposed to ocean, or "blue water") combat. Here, Stauffer sketched USS *Eastport*, an ironclad gunboat destroyed in the disastrous Red River campaign of March–May 1864, as well as the sternwheel steamer *Argosy*, the sidewheel steamer *Avenger*, and the ironclad gunboat *Essex*.

36 | PICTURES OF THE CIVIL WAR

Stauffer was fascinated with aspects of daily life and architectural styles with which he was not familiar. Pages of this sketchbook and his later ones are filled with realistic depictions of buildings and individuals he saw in his travels.

Depictions of African Americans by most 19th-century artists, particularly in political cartoons, caricaturized blacks' physical appearances, reflecting the deep-seated racism prevalent at the time. Stauffer appears to have created his sketches based on direct observation of individuals and captioned his images using the local patois.

38 | PICTURES OF THE CIVIL WAR

Stauffer's ship, USS *Alexandria*, operated between Donaldsonville, Louisiana, and Mound City, Illinois, the site of shipyards and a large Union hospital. Stauffer appeared more interested in Romeo Park, a local bar, than these facilities. He also sketched a fort in Arkansas and soldiers cleaning the deck, the one on his knees "holystoning" it, in sailors' parlance.

This unknown sailor—possibly Stauffer—relaxes near a cannon aboard a steamer, a pipe in hand and a barrel of rye behind him.

40 | PICTURES OF THE CIVIL WAR

John Worthington Mansfield
1849–1933

New York, New York

Headquarters Division, Third Brigade, Third Division, 24th Army Corps, February–April 1865

In February 1865, fifteen-year-old John Worthington Mansfield most likely lied about his age to join the Union army, having only recently moved with his father to New York City from Chelsea, Massachusetts. Mansfield was stationed at Chapin's Farm near Richmond, Virginia, in a brigade with some soldiers from Chelsea, including Captain Jesse J. Underhill. Mansfield presented Underhill's wife, whom he met in camp, with two sketchbooks entitled "A Trip to the Army of the James." Selections from the third sketchbook created while he was in the military, "Book of Military Scraps," are reprinted here. Mansfield drew many scenes he hadn't witnessed, including the interior of the captain's quarters on the *Monitor*, as well as detailed sketches of ordinary wartime objects. He seemed to be honing his technique throughout this sketchbook, sometimes appearing to be completing a homework assignment.

Mansfield's earliest surviving work is a watercolor of a rose he completed when he was seven. After returning from Virginia in mid-April 1865 after Lee's surrender at Appomattox, he attended art school in New York until 1867. Mansfield was in Paris for most of the 1870s, funded by his father and a Mrs. Josiah Quincy, attached to the Atelier Bonnat. Mansfield returned to New York in 1876 after his father's money ran out and continued to paint in watercolor and oil, including many beautiful oil paintings of Niagara Falls. In 1885, Mansfield moved to Boston to teach at the New England Conservancy of Fine Arts, and in 1887, he set up in Ipswich, Massachusetts, where he remained for the rest of his life. Mansfield exhibited works at the National Academy of Design, the New York Society of Etchers, and the Boston Art Club.

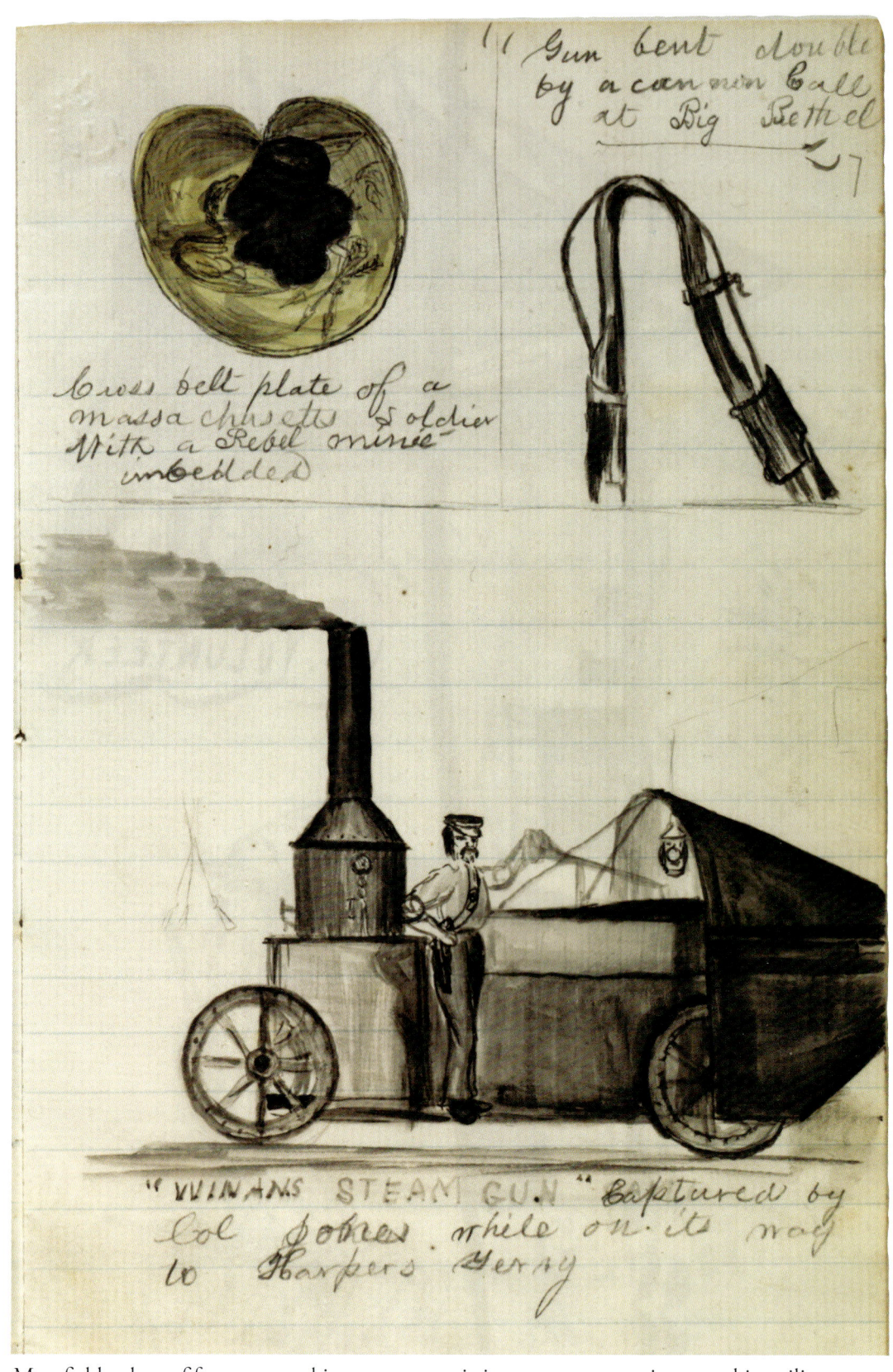

Mansfield, who at fifteen was on his way to an artistic career, was very interested in military technology and the destruction it wrought on objects. Here, he carefully drew a cross belt plate (a favorite target of sharpshooters) with a bullet hole; a gun bent by a cannon ball; and a steam gun captured by Union forces. This image and the ones that follow in this section are from the Gilder Lehrman Collection, GLC09041.

Mansfield's "U.S. Volunteer" stands in stark contrast to the "Rebel" below, with the healthy looking Union soldier facing off against his gaunt, disheveled, ghostly adversary.

Mansfield continued his study of military technology and its destructive forces on this page, drawing a shrapnel-damaged dime, ammunition, and cannons.

Mansfield was twelve and in Massachusetts during the battle of Antietam, but he drew his own version of it. Like Frank Park, he depicted the aftermath of the battle, breaking from the famous scene by Currier & Ives, which takes place in the midst of the fighting. On another page, also reprinted above, Mansfield drew USS *Merrimac*, which he noted was "blown up at Hampton Va by the Rebs."

Continuing to draw what he hadn't seen, Mansfield sketched USS *Monitor*, which sank off Cape Hatteras, N.C., in late 1862. Here, Mansfield imagined the captain and a sailor relaxing in the captain's quarters.

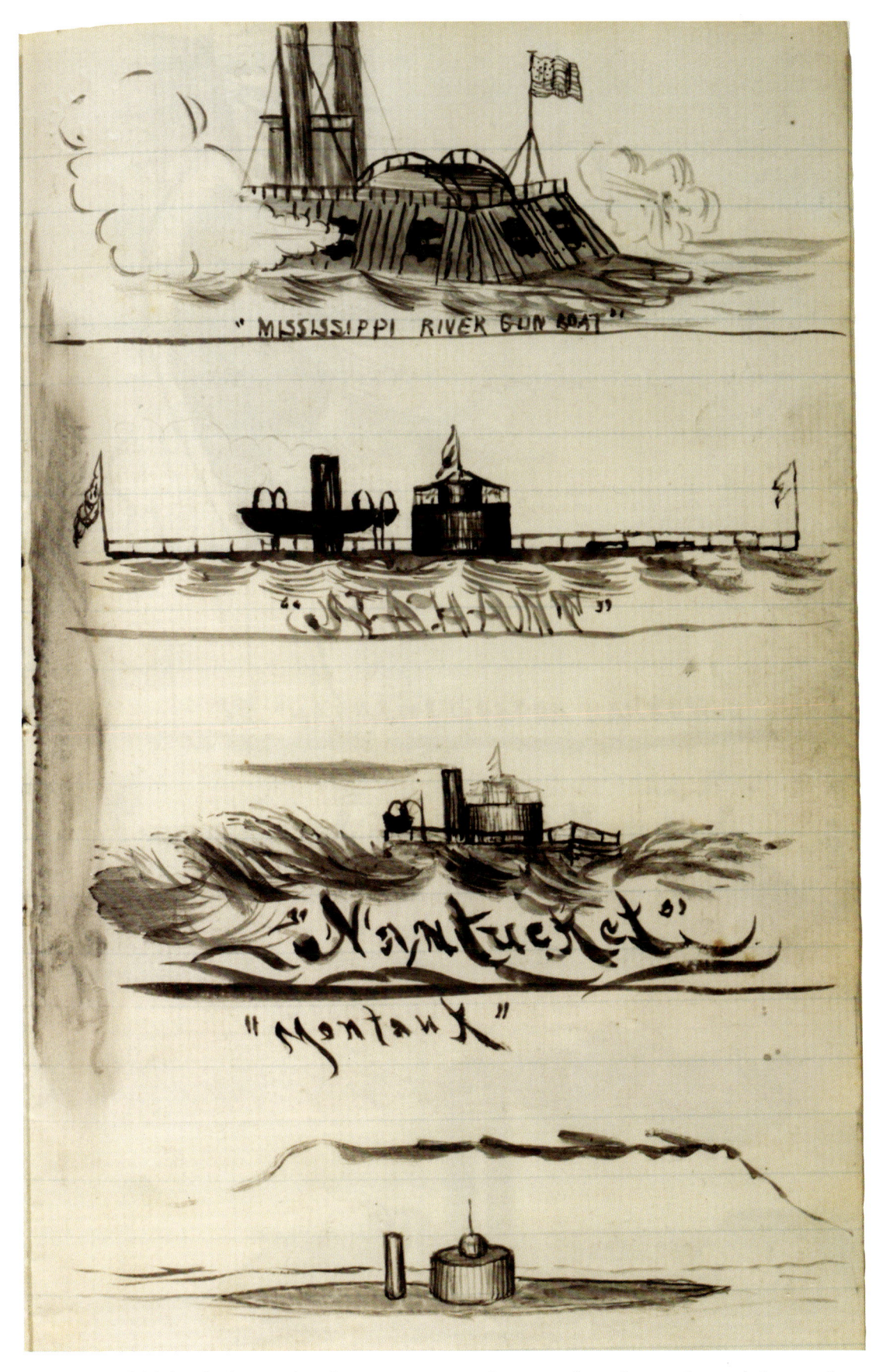

Here, Mansfield sketched more ships he may or may not have seen from the war that ended soon after he enlisted.

Influences on the Artists

Departure scene, Henry Berckhoff

DEPARTURE OF THE 7TH REGT N.Y.S.M. FRIDAY APRIL 19TH 1861. VIEW OF BROADWAY, COR. COURTLAND ST.

Marching to the seat of war May 1861

The departure of the Seventh New York Volunteer Militia regiment for Washington, D.C., on April 19, 1861, just a week after the attack on Fort Sumter, was met with a great patriotic display on the streets of Manhattan. The *New York Times* described the crowds that lined the parade route: "Cortlandt-street showed a gathering of flags, a perfect army of them. . . . It was flag, flag, from every window from the first floor to the roof, from every doorway — in short, it was flag, flag, — and of quite large sizes, too, till the wearied eye refused the task of counting them." The engravers Sarony, Major and Knapp captured the scene on Broadway and Cortlandt Street in a print that sold many copies, and that may have influenced Henry Berckhoff, whose Eighth New York Volunteer regiment followed a similar parade route five weeks later. Berckhoff's "Marching to the seat of war" is set twenty blocks north of Cortlandt Street, at the corner of Spring Street and Broadway, and shows large crowds of New Yorkers turning out to send off their departing heroes. The similarities between the print and Berckhoff's choice of perspective and details are striking.

"Departure of the 7th Regt N.Y.S.M Friday April 19th 1861," lithography by Sarony, Major and Knapp, c. 1861. (The Gilder Lehrman Institute of American History, GLC09118p17; GLC06106p1)

48 | PICTURES OF THE CIVIL WAR

Newspaper headlines, Creator of "George"

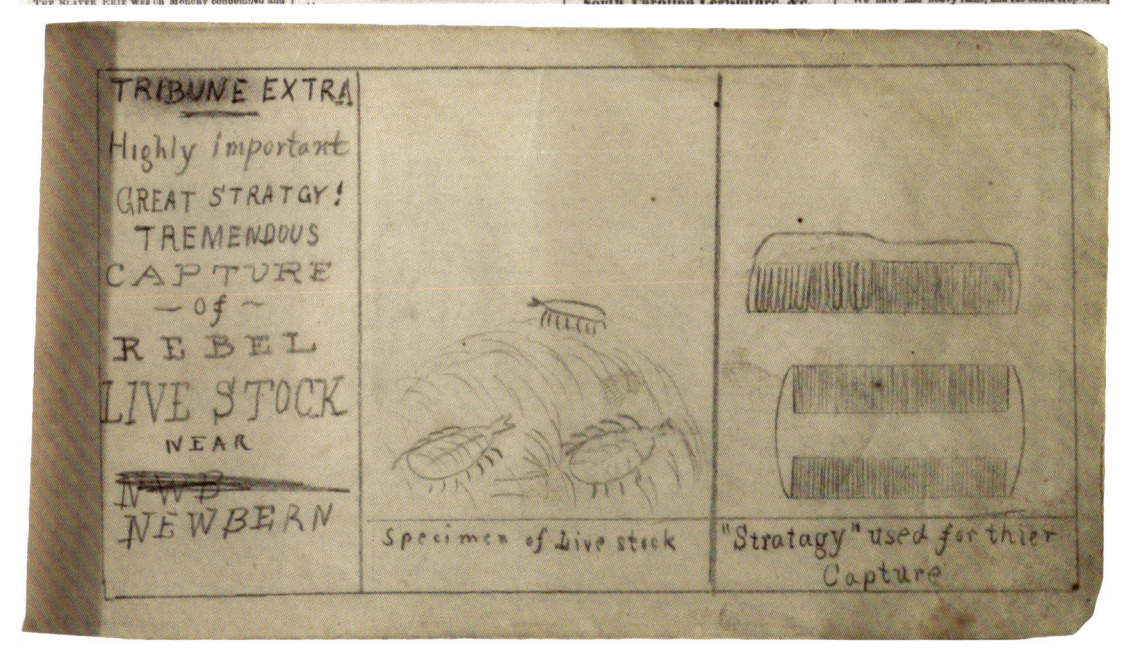

Based on the image reprinted here and similar ones on earlier pages, the creator of the George sketches took some of his inspiration from contemporary newspapers. The headlines on this November 1860 *New York Tribune* front page are typical of the time, with multiple lines of text, or decks, most in a different font and each packed with facts. Our mystery artist imitated these typographical conventions in several sketches and imagined the real story behind the often exaggerated war headlines in clever panels. Here, the "rebel livestock" captured is lice, a scourge of both Union and Confederate soldiers, and the strategy used for their capture them is a comb.

Front page of the Nov. 9, 1860 issue of the *New York Tribune*. (The Gilder Lehrman Institute of American History, GLC08429.09; GLC08200p24)

PICTURES OF THE CIVIL WAR | 49

Battle of Antietam,
Frank Park and
John Mansfield

Antietam, fought on September 17, 1862, was the bloodiest one-day battle of the Civil War. Nearly 6,500 soldiers died, and the retreating Confederates left thousands of their comrades behind where they had fallen. Two days after the battle, professional photographers Alexander Gardner and James Gibson arrived and began taking pictures. According to James McPherson, author of *Antietam: Crossroads of Freedom*, their battlefield photographs of corpses were the first such images most Americans had ever seen, and they had a profound effect. It is very likely that Frank Park and John Mansfield saw many images of Antietam's devastation, though they had not participated in the battle or seen the Sharpsburg, Maryland, battlefield. Park rendered the day's destruction in a symbolic watercolor, depicting skulls, spent cannonballs, and the flag in a scene offering "repose" to the fallen, a stark contrast to the Gardner photograph reprinted here. Mansfield imagined a chaotic fight, with wounded soldiers being carried off the field in agony amidst explosions, in juxtaposition with Currier & Ives's orderly charge.

"The Battle of Antietam, Md. September 17th 1862," lithograph by Currier and Ives, c. 1862. (The Gilder Lehrman Institute of American History, GLC02881.31); GLC09041p13-14. Facing page: A closer view of the field of Antietam, photograph, c. 1862. (The Gilder Lehrman Collection, GLC05111.01.0887; GLC03537p25)

PICTURES OF THE CIVIL WAR | 51

To Learn More

Low resolution images from all five soldiers' sketchbooks are available on the Gilder Lehrman Institute's website. Visit www.gilderlehrman.org, select "Search the Collection" from the "Historic Documents" drop-down menu, and type in the Gilder Lehrman Collection number for each sketchbook, below, in the "Call Number" field.

Henry Berckhoff: GLC06106
A FEW SCENES: GLC08200
Frank E. Park: GLC03537
David McNeely Stauffer: GLC07713.01
John W. Mansfield: GLC09041

BOOKS

Bonner, Robert E. *The Soldier's Pen: Firsthand Impressions of the Civil War*. New York: Hill & Wang, 2006.

Burton, William L. *Melting Pot Soldiers: The Union's Ethnic Regiments*. New York: Fordham University Press, 1998.

Fahs, Alice. *The Imagined Civil War: Popular Literature of the North & South, 1861-1865*. Chapel Hill: University of North Carolina Press, 2001.

Joiner, Gary D. *Mr. Lincoln's Brown Water Navy: The Mississippi Squadron*. Lanham, MD: Rowman & Littlefield Publishers, 2007.

Harris, William C., ed. *"In the Country of the Enemy": The Civil War Reports of a Massachusetts Corporal*. Gainesville: The University of Florida Press, 1999.

McPherson, James M. *Antietam: Crossroads of Freedom*. New York: Oxford University Press, 2002.

Neely, Mark E., Jr., Gabor Boritt and Harold Holzer. *The Confederate Image: Prints of the Lost Cause*. Chapel Hill: The University of North Carolina Press, 1987.

Neely, Mark E., Jr., and Harold Holzer. *The Union Image: Popular Prints of the Civil War North*. Chapel Hill: The University of North Carolina Press, 2000.

Sandweiss, Martha, ed. *Photography in Nineteenth-Century America*. Fort Worth, TX: Amon Carter Museum and New York: Harry N. Abrams, Inc., 1991.

Acknowledgements

Pictures of the Civil War: Five Union Soldiers' Sketchbooks was developed at the Gilder Lehrman Institute by Caroline Luther, education coordinator, and Susan F. Saidenberg, director of exhibitions and public programs. We are grateful to editors Justine Ahlstrom and Elaine Bleakney, and to Sandra Trenholm, director of the Gilder Lehrman Collection, on deposit at the New-York Historical Society; thanks also to Barbara Leff and William Toth of the Monk Design Group. The Henry Berckhoff chapter is partially based on the exhibition *The Civil War in Color: A Soldier's Sketchbook*, curated by Leslie Fields, at the Pierpont Morgan Library Museum from May to September, 1999.

Particular thanks to our funders: The Altman Foundation, Anonymous, Bloomberg LP, The Louis Calder Foundation, David Cuming, Anthony and Christine de Nicola, The Eris and Larry Field Foundation, McInerney Family Foundation, Jean and William Soman, and above all to the founders of the Institute, Richard Gilder and Lewis E. Lehrman, whose generosity makes possible all programs at the Gilder Lehrman Institute.